Table of Contents

Introductiion

Any gardener knows that having the right soil can make all the difference in achieving great results in the garden.Unfortunately, not every garden is blessed with nutrient-dense, high-quality soil. Raised bed gardening is the perfect solution. Using raised beds, you can control your soil and learn to grow beautiful flowers, fruits and vegetables. Even if you don't have a lot of time for gardening, you can still have a productive vegetable garden, no matter the size. How? Start with a raised bed.It's the shortcut to a plentiful harvest, even in the first year.

Here's why:

- Garden anywhere. Attractive cedar raised beds are an asset to your landscape. Create perimeter gardens, spice up your entryway, grow food in your front yard, screen an eyesore.

- More food in less space. You can set plants closer together so every square inch is productive. And small-space gardening techniques, such as succession planting and vertical supports, ensure that every square inch of space is used.

- Plant earlier. Excess water drains better and soil warms up faster in spring compared to in-ground beds. Specialized covers and garden fabric help you get started even earlier.
- Better soil. A productive vegetable garden depends on good soil. With a raised bed, you start fresh with the ideal soil blend even if the soil on your site is poor.

Adding Soil Acidifier

Adding acidifier lowers soil pH for blue hydrangeas, azaleas, and other acid-loving plants.

Fewer weeds. Because raised beds are densely planted, weeds have little room to grow. And when they do find space, it's easy to pull them from the loose, rich soil.

Easier pest control. It's simpler to manage insects and exclude animal pests compared to long garden rows. You can easily cover beds with row fabrics or specialized covers.

Match soil to plants. Fill the beds with soil customized to plants. For example, do you want to grow blue hydrangeas? Mix a soil acidifier into the soil prior to planting.

Less bending to tend. Deep Root Raised beds are 15" high, so you bend less during planting, caring for, and harvesting plants.

Things To Think About Before Preparing A Raised Bed Garden

1. What size will it be?

Raised beds are generally three to four feet wide by about six to eight feet long. This allows you to easily reach into the raised bed from the side to plant and dig and weed, without having to step into the garden where you risk compacting the soil.

The height can also be important. If you are putting your raised bed on a hard surface, like a driveway, or over hard-packed soil, you want to make sure it's deep enough for plants (especially root vegetables like beets and carrots) to root. If it's too shallow those roots will reach down into that subsoil (or hard surface) and hit a brick wall. I usually recommend at least 10 to 12 inches.

2. How do you pick the perfect spot?

When preparing a raised bed garden, location is everything, but it doesn't have to be your backyard. Your raised bed could go in a sunny side yard, your front yard, or even your driveway.

3. How will you get rid of grass?

Good question because this is a common concern. If you've ever tried to cut out and lift sod, you know what an enormous task it is. An easier way to get rid of grass is to outline the space and cover it with a layer of cardboard and cover that with a layer of soil. The grass will break down and voilà! A new garden site. Doing this in the fall will allow everything to break down over the winter.

4. Do you want to install irrigation?

If you want to set up a whole drip irrigation system with a line running from your tap or rain barrel, you might want to do this before your raised bed areas are finished and filled. That way you can run hoses under pathways or layers of mulch, and adapt the bed around where the hose attaches to the irrigation system.

5. How much soil will you need and what kind?

There are some handy soil calculators out there that will help you determine how much you need to fill your raised bed, like this one from Gardener's Supply Company.

As far as type of soil, I like to emphasize buying the best quality that you can afford when preparing a raised bed garden. When I had multiple raised beds to fill, I ordered triple mix from a local supplier (after chatting with them on the phone about my options) and top-dressed it with organic vegetable compost. I like to recommend leaving some in reserve to replenish your raised beds throughout the season. Please visit this link if you want more details on the best soil for raised beds.

6. Should you stake the sides?

One thing I wish that I had done when I built my first two raised beds is install a couple of midpoint stakes to prevent the beds from shifting over time. This is one of my number one raised bed tips!

Not sure how many vegetables you can grow in each one of your beds? Here are several illustrated 4×8 raised bed layout plans you can use to determine the placement and spacing of your veggie plants.

Raised Beds

A raised bed is basically a large, above-ground planter, with walls ranging from 6-24 inches high. Generally these beds are encased in some sort of frame usually wood, concrete or stone. Once the housing for the bed is built, it is filled with soil forming a simple, but effective planter. If the area where the bed is constructed has poor soil quality, outside soil can be used.

Raised beds can be used to grow just about anything. They make great vegetable planters, can be a lovely way to display flowers and are an ideal choice for shrubbery, fruits and herbs. When properly constructed, raised beds can be a beautiful way to create distinguished planting areas in the garden.

Choosing a Raised Bed

Gardener's Supply offers a wide range of raised beds, from aluminum corner kits for which you supply your own lumber, to complete raised bed kits in cedar, composite wood, recycled plastic and galvanized steel. You can also consider elevated raised beds, for no-bend gardening.

Forever Raised Bed

Our Forever Raised Beds can be set up in minutes and last for decades. Made from a composite of recycled wood and plastic, they have the attractive look and feel of silvery aged cedar, but will never splinter or rot.

Raised beds range in height, starting at about 6". In general, the more soil depth that's available to your plants, the more freely their roots will grow. More soil also holds more moisture, so a deeper raised bed will require less frequent watering.

It is possible to install a raised bed on poor or compacted soil, or even on concrete. If this is the situation you have, buy the deepest bed you can afford. A depth of 10-12" is preferable. Keep in mind that the deeper the bed, the more soil you'll need to fill it. Use the Soil Calculator to determine how much soil you'll need.

How many raised beds should you have? If your space or time is limited, you might want to start out with just one. If you're trying to produce lots of your own fresh vegetables, you will probably need at least three or four beds. Use the Kitchen Garden Planner, our free online garden design tool, to select and place the crops you want to have in each bed. This will help you determine how many total beds you'll need to accommodate everything you want to grow.

Location and Set-up

For optimum plant health and productivity, most vegetables should receive at least eight hours of full sun each day. The more sun, the better, so it makes sense to locate your garden in the sunniest part of your yard. Avoid low, wet areas where the soil could stay soggy. Because your garden will need to be watered during the growing season, you'll want to have relatively easy access to a hose.

Good soil is the single most important ingredient for a good garden. Raised beds give you an immediate advantage over a regular garden, because when you fill your raised bed, you can fill it with a blend of soil that's superior to the native soil in your yard. Soil that's loose and rich with nutrients and organic matter will allow the roots of your plants to grow freely, and ensure that they have access to the water and nutrients they need to sustain healthy growth.

Before placing your raised beds in their permanent location, be sure to remove grass or perennial weeds from the area. Use a garden fork or shovel to loosen the native soil to a depth of 6-10". This will improve drainage and moisture retention in the raised beds. It also means that even with a 5"-high raised bed, your plants will think they're growing in a bed that's 12-18" deep — plenty of room for carrots, potatoes, full-size tomato plants and most any other vegetable you'd ever want to grow.

If you'll be filling more than one raised bed, you might want to buy your soil in bulk — by the cubic foot or cubic yard. Use the Soil Calculator to figure out the total amount of soil you'll need for each bed. For most situations, we recommend these proportions:

- 60% topsoil
- 30% compost
- 10% Potting soil (a soilless growing mix that contains peat moss, perlite and/or vermiculite)

Shop For Potting Soil

Keep in mind that proportions are approximate because soil volume varies from source to source. For instance, if the calculator specifies .444 cubic yards of soil for your bed, go ahead and buy a half yard.

If you do not have access to quality topsoil, an acceptable substitute would be a 50-50 blend of soilless growing medium (often called "potting soil") and compost. If you want to add peat moss to the bed, it should not be more than 20 percent of the total mix. Peat moss is naturally acidic and is not a good medium for growing vegetables.

What To Plant

Fill your garden with the types of vegetables you like to eat. If you're big on salads, plant head lettuce, a lettuce cutting mix, cherry tomatoes, cucumbers and carrots. If you love cooking, plant onions and peppers, leeks, potatoes and herbs. Try to include at least one vegetable that's new to you. Discovery is half the fun.

Tomatillos and tomatoes

Choose vegetables that you like to eat — or try something that's new to you.

Gardening in a raised bed is all about maximizing productivity. The challenge is to grow as much food as possible while resisting the temptation to squeeze in too many plants. Overcrowded plants never reach their full potential because they're stressed by poor air circulation and competition for water, nutrients and root space.

It's also important consider how each plant's growth habit (bushy, climbing, trailing) will affect its neighbors in same the bed. Planting lettuce next to carrots is fine; planting lettuce next to a sprawling cucumber plant may be a problem. Stakes, ladders and cages will help keep unruly plants from competing with their neighbors. They will also keep the garden neater and more manageable.

Though most of the vegetables you'll want to grow could be started directly in the garden from seed, in many cases it's best to start out with a plant. Starting with a plant usually shortens the time to harvest by a month or more. In cold regions, where the growing season may be less than 100 days, a tomato or pepper plant that's started in the garden from seed will not have time to mature before frost. When you're putting in just one or two plants of a particular type of vegetable (such as broccoli or tomatoes), it sometimes makes more sense to purchase a couple plants rather than invest in an entire packet of seeds.

Vegetables that can be sown directly into the garden from seed include root crops, such as carrots and beets, beans, peas, corn, cucumbers, squash and salad greens. In some cases, these crops are direct-sown because they do not transplant well and it's best to sow the seeds right where they're going to grow. In the case of salad greens, which germinate well and grow quickly, it is simply more economical to purchase a packet of seeds than to purchase multiple six-packs of lettuce seedlings.

Potatoes can be started from seed but almost nobody does so. It's much faster and easier to grow a new potato plant from a tuber rather than from a seed. Onions can be put into the garden as seeds, but more often they go in as plants or as "sets", which are simply tiny mature onions from the prior growing season. For more information, on choosing seeds, seedlings or sets, read Growing Onions. Garlic and shallots are usually planted from sets as well. Leeks go into the garden as young plants. Some herbs should be put in as plants, some (cilantro and dill) should be seeded right where they are to grow.

When To Plant

There are several factors to consider when deciding when to plant your garden. First is the type of plant you're putting in. Some plants, including lettuce and broccoli, can tolerate cool weather. Others, such as basil and tomatoes, are likely to be damaged or killed by temperatures lower than 40 degrees. Refer to our Vegetable Encyclopedia to determine the best time to plant each crop.

Other important considerations are frost dates and soil temperature. In planting zones 3 to 6, the primary gardening season falls between the first and last frost dates. Cold-sensitive plants must not go into the garden until all danger of frost has passed. This typically falls somewhere between March and May, depending on your growing zone. If you don't know your growing zone, check the USDA zone map.

If you garden in zones 8-10, it may be heat — not frost — that determines your planting dates. Warm-climate gardeners often plant in the fall rather than the spring, to avoid midsummer heat. Others gear up for two planting periods each year: early fall and late winter.

Soil temperature is also an important planting-time consideration. Most plants thrive in a moderate soil temperature of 60 to 70 degrees F. Some, such as peas and spinach, will germinate well and grow just fine in cool (45 degrees F.) soil. Others, such as eggplant and melons, will not germinate, nor will they grow properly unless the soil is above 60 degrees F. The Vegetable Encyclopedia has planting recommendations for each crop.

Some vegetables, including tomatoes, peppers, squash and corn, are typically planted just once each growing season. Other crops, such as salad greens, roots crops, peas and beans, can be planted and harvested early, and then be planted again later in the season for a second harvest. The Vegetable Encyclopedia has crop-specific recommendations for planting (and replanting) to help you maximize production.

Once the seeds have been planted, the area should be watered thoroughly, to a depth of several inches. The soil should be kept consistently moist until the seeds germinate and the young plants have established their first sets of true leaves. Most seeds have a hard coating that must be softened for a period of several days before the seedling inside can emerge. If the soil dries out during this time, the process will be interrupted and you may need to reseed. Covering newly planted areas with garden fabric (or shade netting in the summer) helps keep the top layer of soil consistently moist. This cover can be removed once the seedlings are up and the plants are established.

If possible, young seedlings should be transplanted into the garden when the weather is calm, cool and drizzly. Tender seedlings will suffer if they're planted out on a sunny, hot or windy day. If the weather doesn't cooperate, water your new seedlings thoroughly after planting and then cover them with garden fabric for several days. The plants need time to establish new roots before they are able to extract moisture and nutrients from the soil. If you do not cover them with garden fabric, you may want to find another way to shield them from the sun and drying wind. Be sure to water these new plants every day or two for the first couple weeks.

Tending Your Garden

Planting intensively keeps weeds to a minimum. In the early spring you may need to weed a little every week, but by midsummer your weeding chores should be over. When weeds do crop up, you'll want to remove them quickly so your vegetable plants aren't competing for moisture, nutrients and root space.

The soil in a raised bed doesn't dry out as fast as it does in a regular garden. The sides of the bed help retain moisture and the plants shade the soil to reduce evaporation. Once plants are well-established, your watering chores should be minimal except in hot weather and periods of drought.

Crops that grow take three or four months to mature usually benefit from a second, midseason application of fertilizer. Almost all vegetables appreciate a monthly dose of water-soluble fertilizer, especially one that includes humic acid, seaweed and fish emulsion. These water-soluble nutrients are immediately absorbed by plants and help keep them healthy in periods of stress. This is an easy way to minimize pest and disease problems.

You can begin harvesting food from your garden just as soon as it looks ready to eat. Crops are usually tastiest and most nutritious at or just before their peak of ripeness. Remove any spent fruit or foliage, as well as any damaged or diseased plant material. Keep an eye out for pests and address any issues promptly (our Pest and Disease Directory can help you identify potential problems).

Some plants, including pole beans and most tomatoes, need a cage, trellis or another type of support to grow properly and produce a good crop. Plant supports also save space, help keep the garden neat and make it easier to access plants for harvesting.

Tomato Cage Ladders

Increase productivity by using vegetable supports, such as tomato cages and ladders.

You will also need to fertilize your plants to keep them healthy and maximize productivity.We recommend using a granular, all-purpose organic fertilizer at planting time and again midseason. You may also want to have some garden fabric (row covers) for transplanting and frost protection, plant ties, and a watering wand or watering can. For more ideas, see all of our products for raised bed gardening.

Watering

In a perfect world, Mother Nature would provide an inch of rain each week to keep our vegetables and flowers perfectly happy. Because that's probably not going to happen, it's up to us to make sure our plants get the water they need to thrive.

A rain gauge will help you keep track of how much rain has fallen, but that's really only part of the story. Different types of soil have different abilities to hold water. A clay-based soil holds onto water because each little particle of clay has lots of surface area for the water to grab onto. Sandy soil, with its bigger particles, lets water pass through quickly. A good loamy soil retains some moisture, yet is also well-drained.

Adding compost to the soil improves its ability to supply your plants with just the right amount of water. Think of sandy soil like a wire basket full of golf balls: turn the hose on and the water runs right through. Adding compost is like adding sponges — water still runs through, but some is stored in the sponges. Compost also helps improve clay soils by aerating them and providing better drainage. Plants absorb oxygen through their roots and can drown if the soil stays soggy for weeks at a time. Raised beds and compost can help prevent this from happening.

The best way to monitor soil moisture is with your hands. When you stick a finger down into the soil, it should feel lightly damp — like a sponge that has been wrung out. Don't just feel the surface; get your fingers down to the root zone (3" deep or so) at least once a week.

In hot weather, plants may wilt during the heat of the day. This isn't always an indication that they're moisture-deprived. In many cases it's simply a way for the plant to reduce moisture loss through its leaves. Checking the soil tells the real story.

Planting intensively in a raised bed garden minimizes moisture loss. Plants shade the soil surface and help protect one another from the wind. Mulching around plants with 2-3" of shredded leaves or straw is another effective way to retain moisture and add organic matter to the soil.

If you determine that your garden does need water, there are several options. A watering wand will deliver quite a bit of water quickly, and get it right where you want it. Too busy to water during the week? Going on vacation in August? Buy a water timer to automatically turn on a sprinkler or soaker hose. Soaker hoses and drip irrigation systems with emitters leak water slowly right at soil level, and are a very efficient way to water.

To keep your plants healthy and productive, don't let the soil dry out completely. If delicate root hairs die back, the plant must direct its energy to re-growing them, rather than to producing fruit. Water-stressed plants can also become bitter and tough.

Pros of Raised Beds

There are many benefits to creating this type of garden bed. One great benefit is that you can determine which type of soil to fill the planter with, which gives you complete control over soil quality and nutrition. This can be a big help if your backyard soil is composed of sand or heavy clay. Raised beds also extend your growing season because they warm much earlier in the spring. This will allow for earlier planting and cultivation in the garden. They promote good soil drainage and will help you to achieve the ideal water balance for each of your plants.

Another great benefit of the raised garden bed is the ease of access. Most gardeners plan the width of their beds carefully (usually no more than 4 feet) to ensure that the entire planting area is accessible from the sides. This can make gardening easier for those that have a hard time kneeling to plant and weed their garden. Raised beds, correctly designed, can even be accessed by those in wheelchairs. The raised design also keeps you from compacting your soil and crushing plants.

Cons of Raised Beds

Raised beds are a convenient gardening option, but they aren't without their downfalls. One downside is that they must generally be cultivated by hand. Garden tillers are almost impossible to use in a raised bed. However, if you continue to amend the soil with quality compost, your soil should remain workable with little digging needed. Another con is the initial time and expense required for installation of these beds. Whether you choose to build the beds on your own or to use a pre-made kit, they can be costly and will take time to set up and properly install.

Placing Your Beds

The placement of your beds is very important and will depend on what you wish to grow. For example, tomatoes require at least 8 hours of direct sunlight, while shade-loving plants prefer minimal sun. Determine what you will be planting and then find a location that will provide the ideal light and growing conditions. Also consider its ease of access from your home, location of your water supply, and proximity to pests like deer and rabbits.

The area will also need to be properly prepared before planting can begin. One of the first things that you will want to do is remove any weeds and vegetation from the bed site. This can be accomplished through manual digging to remove the sod and get down to bare soil. Covering the area with black plastic sheeting or a thick layer of mulch for several months will make your job much easier. If you are building a tall raised bed (12 inches or more) you can leave grass in place, put some newspaper or paper bags down to smother the grass, and simply add the soil on top. The paper will simply disintegrate in a couple months. If your yard is plagued by burrowing animals like moles, you may want to consider putting chicken wire in the bottom of the bed — but whatever you do, make sure earthworms can get into your beds to keep the soil healthy.

Building A Raised Garden Bed?

Building a raised garden bed is a pretty simple process if you have the right tools and a plan in place before you get started.

You can by raised bed kits from garden supply centers, or you can build your own from scratch. The first thing that you will want to do is choose the materials that you will use to construct your bed. You can use almost anything from wood to concrete to stone and even materials found around the home. When choosing your materials, it is important to consider what chemicals could be leached into the soil. Non-toxic materials are especially important when growing vegetables or other edible plants since any chemicals in the soil can pass into the produce.

Once you have determined which materials to use, you can get started with the construction process. Take the time to make your frame stable and secure since this will help it to last and will limit soil erosion. Once the frame is constructed it should be filled with soil. This is a great opportunity for you to create a soil mix that will help your plants to prosper, so choose a soil that is ideal for the type of plants that you are planning on growing. Mixing sand into your soil will improve your drainage and using an organic matter like peat moss or compost will help the soil retain optimal moisture levels.

Planting Tips

Once your beds are constructed they are ready for planting. You can plant a variety of different fruits, vegetables and floral accents in the same bed or you can separate various types of plants.

Think about plant placement: Tall plants should be planted in the middle of your bed or along one side so that they don't block access to other plants or create unwanted shade.

Pay attention to planting guidelines: Raised beds will be ready for spring planting earlier than non-raised beds. Follow the specific planting guidelines for each plant you choose. Plant too early and your plants may freeze, but plant too late in the season and you may not have enough time for produce to fully develop before the season is over.

Fertilizer is important: Proper fertilizing of your plants will help your plants to grow. When applying fertilizer try to apply around the base of the plant and to avoid contact with the plants leaves.

Weed and Pest Management

Raised beds are easier to maintain than ground level beds, but they still require regular maintenance. You can use mulch to keep weeds at bay and row or bed covers for pest management. Since raised beds are self contained they are often easier to cover than other styles of garden beds.

1. What size will it be?

Raised beds are generally three to four feet wide by about six to eight feet long. This allows you to easily reach into the raised bed from the side to plant and dig and weed, without having to step into the garden where you risk compacting the soil.

Common Garden Pests and Prevention Methods

- Aphids
- Whitefly
- Mealybug
- Thrips
- Cabbage Looper

1. Aphids

These are small, common garden pests that suck the sap from your plants. Due to their size, it can be difficult to identify aphids in small numbers, often only being noticed once a plant is infested. Once infested, aphids can quickly damage and kill plants.

Aphids can be many colors, including green, black or pink. They target newly growing, soft plants to feed on. When aphids multiply, they begin fighting over position they can be found on the plant's stem, under leaves, even on the fruit.

As aphids feed and multiple, a sticky honeydew is generated that increases mold growth. Aphids commonly produce winged generations which fly off to the next garden.

Signs of Aphids

- Sticky residue on plants
- Mold growth
- Reduced plant quality
- Small spots on plants (can look like tiny dots)

Prevention Methods

Many gardeners will regularly check their plants, ready to pinch off any aphids before they multiply. However, due to their size and not all of us have 20/20 vision, there are some other ways to reduce these garden pests.

- Aphids can usually be removed with a good hosing or using a spray bottle to knock them off plants.
- Increase native parasites and predators to manage aphids. These include: lacewings, aphid midges, and lady bugs.

- Using floating row cover plants, when possible.
- Spray plants with garlic or hot pepper repellants (ensure repellant will not damage your plants first, of course).

Application of insecticidal soap, horticultural oil or neem.

2. Whitefly

The whitefly appears similar to a white 'moth', but is not actually a fly. Whiteflies are more related to aphids and hide under the leaves which make them a challenge to manage. To increase this challenge, whiteflies can quickly multiple. During the summer, a whitefly matures from egg to adult in about 16 days.

How The Whitefly Damages Your Plants

Direct Damage: This is caused from sucking sap directly from the plants. This will cause yellowing and shriveling leaves. When there are multiple whiteflies, it can kill plants.

Indirect Damage: The adult whitefly may transmit various viruses between a diseased and healthy plant. Like aphids, the whitefly secrets "honeydew", which leaves sticky residue on plants.This honeydew aids in fungus growth known as "sooty mold", which result in leaves appearing dirty and black.Although harmless itself, it prevents sun from reaching plant surfaces, increasing plant stress.

Signs Of Whiteflies

The most common way to identify these garden pests is by disturbing plants – whiteflies will flutter around.

Whitefly nymphs (prior to growing their wings) have oval bodies.

Prevention Methods

The best organic method to prevent whiteflies, like with other common garden pests, is to understand beneficial insects. For example, parasitic wasps use the body of whiteflies for laying eggs, which kills the whitefly and parasitic wasps are unable to sting people.

- Plant flowering plants that attract beneficial insects and natural predators, including spiders, ladybugs, and lacewings.
- Place sticky traps around the garden for early detection.
- Always inspect new plants before purchasing, avoid buying plants that are infected.

Already Got a Whitefly Infestation?

Here are a few ways to gain control of your garden:

- Spray plants with a stream of water to remove whiteflies and honeydew. When done in early morning, the adult whitefly will be slower, use a vacuum to capture fluttering whiteflies. Empty the vacuum into a sealable plastic bag and discard.
- Prune and discard of severely infested parts of plants.
- Increase beneficial insects, such lady bugs. A single black lady bug (Delphastus) is able to consume 150 whitefly eggs per day.

3. Mealybug

These garden pests leave behind a white cotton style coating on plants, which is often the biggest sign you have mealybugs. The mealybug is more common in outdoor gardens located in the south, and houseplants in the north.

Mealybugs have a soft body, which is why they depend on their cotton-style coat to protect them. They are most active when young, and slow down to eat when grown.

The mealybug sucks the sap out of plants, creating a honeydew which they cover themselves in. Their cotton style coat not only protects them from predators, but various control products too. However, with persistence they can be managed.

Signs of Mealybugs

- Sticky residue on plants (honeydew)
- White cotton looking patches

Prevention Methods

The first step is to keep plants healthy, as mealybugs target weak, stressed and hungry plants.

Mealybugs in Small Numbers

Only see a few mealybugs? Use a stream of water to knock them off, similar to aphids and the whitefly. Repeat as needed to control a small issue from becoming a larger problem.

Mealybugs in Large Numbers

When the mealybugs have taken over, it can be harder to eliminate them due to the cotton-style coating, which protects these garden pests from various sprays. However, there are a couple approaches to regain control of your vegetable garden (or rose garden):

Systemic Bug Control

The following products have been known to absorb into the cotton-style coating of mealybugs. Also, they absorb into plant leaves, killing future mealybugs up to 4 weeks:

- Ortho Flower, Fruit & Vegetable Insect Killer
- Ortho Rose & Flower Insect Killer (Ready to Use)

Oil Sprays

This method smothers the mealybugs using a product such as Ortho Fruit Tree Spray.

Note:

Always check to ensure a product is safe for your type of plants before purchasing.

4. Thrips

These garden pests are roughly the size of a sewing needle, and can be found worldwide eating on all types of plants. Depending on the location, they may be referred to as thunderflies or thysanoptera.

Thrips feed on plants by sucking the sap, which can result in plant damage itself. However, the real danger is thrips transmitting viruses between a diseased plant and healthy plant.

Thrips use bark, plant debris or other types of materials to hibernate through winter, becoming active again during early spring, laying eggs within plant tissues. It only takes 3 to 5 days for eggs to hatch, with nymphs feeding on plants for 1 to 3 weeks prior to molting. Depending on the location and weather conditions, Thrips can have up to 15 generations per year.

Without a magnifying glass, it can be hard to detect thrips in early stages, appearing as small dark slivers on the plant. Under a magnifying glass, they have a lobster look to them.

Signs of Thrips

Thrips can range in color, from brown, black, to yellow. Thrips nymphs are often yellow or light green and may have red eyes.

When disturbed, thrips often fly or leap off using fringed, narrow wings.

See dark slivers on plants? Hold a white piece of paper under the plant and try to shake the slivers off, making them easier to see.

Plants have streaks or small white patches.

Prevention Methods

- Use blue or yellow sticky traps for early detection.
- Plant flowers to attract beneficial insects, such as lacewings, lady bugs, and pirate bugs.

Managing Thrips

- Lay cloth under plants, then gently shake plants to jar loose the thrips.
- Use insecticidal soap to kill infestations.
- Apply diatomaceous earth (DE) under leaves–use as a last resort.

Note:

For thrips on fruit trees, spray the trees with dormant oil.

5. Cabbage Looper

These garden pests are common among cabbage plants. They are found throughout the United States, Mexico, even Canada. They look like little green caterpillars. Maintaining control over cabbage loopers is important to prevent holes and rotting spots in your plants.

Larvae of the cabbage looper matures into a thick green caterpillar that has white stripes on the side. The head is thinner than the rest of the body. When fully matured, cabbage loopers can be 2-inches long. After the cabbage looper pupates, it turns into a gray-brown moth.

These pests damage plants as they chew the foliage and leave holes and jagged edges on leaves. Luckily, this common garden pest is large enough to spot visually.

Prevention Methods

- Increase beneficial predators
- Place row covers at time of planting.

Management Methods

The safest way to remove cabbage loopers is by visually inspecting plants and manually removing them. The best time to look is in the early morning or late evening as temperatures are the coolest. Pick off all of them you can see from the plants, and discard of them as you wish. One method is to drop them into hot soapy water.

Inspect under leaves for cabbage looper eggs, gently scrape them off into a container if found. Eggs are laid in ridged rows. Organic cabbage looper pesticides, such as Bacillus thuringiensis (Bt). Try to avoid using chemicals, as they can also kill the beneficial predators.

Which Materials Are Safe For Containing Your Beds?

Size and shape will likely also be dependent on your materials. More importantly, many of you expressed concerns and had questions about which materials are safe. Here's where things can really go sideways. There are so much conflicting information and surprisingly few studies on the various materials available for use.

Why do materials matter? First of all, the materials you use will be in close quarters to your food crop. In all likelihood, the roots and foliage will be regularly making contact with your material surface.

Secondly, the soil you place in your bed will need to remain fairly moist, and the exterior surfaces of your bed will be spending a lot of time in the hot sun. Most materials degrade when exposed to constant moisture and sunlight.

I used 16' lengths of 6"x6" untreated cedar at the GardenFarm but living in the heavily-populated Atlanta area offers me a better supply of wood materials than will be available for many of you.

Regardless, here are pros and cons to the materials you may be considering:

Raw Wood:

The best types of untreated wood are black walnut, cypress, cedar, redwood, oak, black locust, or osage orange. These are known for their rot-resistant properties and last for many years, even under moist conditions.

These woods can be difficult to find available for purchase in some areas. They are also expensive. Untreated pine is a less expensive untreated option, but it will also have a shorter lifespan.

Another consideration: Aside from pine, these woods are not as sustainable as other materials. Often, these woods are harvested from old-growth forest. If you choose to use one of these woods, check that it is coming from a sustainable source. Look for the Forest Stewardship Council (FSC) certification on any wood you buy. The FSC is an international organization that has developed standards for responsible forest management.

All types untreated wood will need to be replaced at some point. The lifespan of your wood will depend on wood type and your environment. If you live in an arid climate, untreated wood can last for several years. If you live in a hot and muggy area, untreated wood may only see you through a couple of years.

Replacing your wood does not signify failure. The untreated wood is decomposing and even adding some nutrients to your garden bed in the process. It's more a matter of maintenance and realistically assessing what will work best for you and your family.

Wood Stains & Paint:

You may opt to extend the life of your untreated wood by staining or painting it. I recommend using a natural treatment like raw linseed oil or raw tung oil.

It's important to look for the raw form of these, as those not marked "raw" will likely include other chemicals. The chemicals are added to speed up the oil drying process, so by using the raw versions, allow for additional drying time.

Another thing to bear in mind is that linseed oil is a food source for mildew, so if mildew is a problem in your area, that may not be a good choice for you.

There haven't been many studies on the impact of using paints or stains for garden bed structure. Paint and stain ingredients vary, and overall, the impact is relatively unknown. But common sense should remind you that these all include chemicals of some nature, and those chemicals may impact your crop.

I recommend against painting the exterior only of your raised bed structure. The wood exposed to the moist soil will wick up moisture, but the exterior paint won't allow the wood to fully "breathe." So by painting the exterior only, you will be trapping the moisture inside and shortening the lifespan of your wood.

Treated Wood:

Treated wood has been infused with chemical elements to preserve the wood. CCA (Chromated Copper Arsenate) wood used to be the most commonly available. The primary concern with treated wood is that those infused elements leach out of the wood. The arsenic in CCA led manufacturers of CCA-treated wood to discontinue its availability for residential applications in 2003.

Although you may find older CCA-treated wood, today's retail options will more likely be ACQ (Ammoniacal Copper Quat) or MCA (Micronized Copper Azole). They have a higher concentration of copper but don't have the arsenic.

Leaching occurs at the highest levels under the following conditions:

- Smaller surfaces – i.e., the ends and – especially, the sawdust

- More recently treated (although CCA-treated wood is shown to retain uniformly-high levels of CCA)
- Moist conditions – i.e., after rain or in a muggy environment
- In unhealthy soil

So to put this into an interesting perspective, studies exploring the impact of treated wood when used for raised beds have shown that the greatest risk is actually in touching the exterior of the bed. When you (or especially, your kids) sit on or lean on treated wood, your skin or clothing is most likely to absorb the copper or arsenic leaching out of the wood to remain on the surface.

If you currently have beds made of the older CCA-treated wood, don't be alarmed. If you're using lots of compost, you should be fine, since plants don't even take up arsenic unless the soil is deficient in phosphorus. And that's likely not the case since phosphorus tends to be immobile and ongoing amendments of compost just add to the overall volume.

In other words, really healthy soil with lots of organic matter does not take up arsenic by plant roots. Yet the more acidic or alkaline your soil, the more likelihood of those elements being taken up by your plants. So, just another reason for getting a soil test to get your soil closer to a neutral pH (6.5-7.0 – also the ideal range for vegetable growth). Ditto for soil with a low amount of organic matter, so make sure your soil analysis tests for organic matter percentage as well.

As for the newer ACQ and MCA treated wood (which have higher copper levels), plants in your food garden won't be able to tolerate high levels of copper, and studies show that healthy soil also prevents uptake of copper.

Even if copper levels are high and being taken up, the plants will die before you ever have a chance to think about eating them. At any rate, that would be a good indicator of a potential problem – in which case you might want to think about having your soil tested for metal concentrations.

While we're on the subject, root vegetables are at greatest risk of being impacted by leaching, as most metals (when taken up) remain in plant roots. Studies further show that those root vegetables are impacted most on their surface. So by thoroughly washing all the impacted soil off and peeling the skin off your potatoes, beets, etc.; you will be eliminating potential contamination.

Your tomatoes and your eggplant could absorb copper or arsenic into their roots, but it is generally not shown to affect the fruit. Leafy greens are an exception and can take up arsenic in their leaves.

In short: Keep your soil near neutral and add lots of compost (more on both of these later), thoroughly wash off the soil and peel the skin from your root vegetables, and avoid contact with the exterior surface of the treated wood. As an extra precaution, grow leafy greens and root vegetables more toward the center of your bed (12” from the perimeter if possible), furthest from the treated wood.

A final note: When building treated wood beds, make your cuts somewhere that allows you to contain the sawdust. Wear a dust mask and gloves, and remove and dispose of the sawdust promptly. Don't add it to your compost.

Cinder or Concrete Blocks:

The truth is, these days the terms are used interchangeably. If your “cinder” blocks are decades old, they may actually be cinder blocks, but only concrete blocks have been in production for the past 50+ years.

What are your concrete blocks made from? That depends somewhat on your area, but there are consistencies. Virtually all concrete blocks are made of what's called Portland cement as well as aggregate, like sand or gravel.

One of the ingredients of Portland cement is fly ash (ranging from 15% to 25%). It's used to make concrete blocks lighter yet stronger. Fly ash is a fine powder byproduct of coal burning, so In other words, it's a petroleum byproduct.

And here's the real rub: fly ash contains various amounts of toxic metals; including arsenic, lead, and mercury. So, yes, those metals are in the concrete blocks that line your vegetable garden too.

Concrete block raised garden bed frame

While that might sound scary, the risk of those metals becoming available in the soil only happens if part of the concrete block is pulverized. Then, it's a matter of several factors that determine the potential risk to what you are growing.

First, the proximity of plant roots to the damaged area. Next, soils higher in organic matter are always beneficial but especially in this case, because they help chemically bind the metals – making them unavailable for absorption into the plant.

Just as with CCA-treated wood, root crops and leafy greens are most susceptible when exposed to higher concentrations.

So, how much fly ash is absorbed by soil held within a concrete block structure? Well, if the block is intact, little to none. But not much research has been done on this specific subject.

If you have beds made from concrete blocks, just avoid anything that would cause them to break to the point that the dust from pulverized pieces can come in contact with plant roots.

And if you really want to "do something," seal the interior lining with a polymer paint (the most practical option), or line the interior side with PE plastic. It's up to you to decide if it's really worth the trouble.

If building raised beds over a concrete surface, the same risks and preventions would apply.

The bottom line: It's not a huge risk, and there are many other ways you are likely taking unintended and harmful materials into your body, far beyond the risk posed by these blocks. That's my opinion, but I do encourage you to do your own research on this if you'd like to learn more. There is so much information out there on the subject, and it will quickly take you in many directions. So, just be mindful of the reliability of the sources of these articles.

Composite Wood:

Composite wood is made of recycled materials and can last for years. Some composite material, when used in long side walls can buckle a bit. Here again, there hasn't been much research on the use of composite wood in proximity to edibles.

Are there any chemicals or elements released by the composite material? It appears to be a benign product for garden use, but there isn't much information out there to make a solid determination.

Galvanized Metal:

There's little scientific information available examining the effect of galvanized metal in the use of raised beds. What I can tell you is that the galvanization process typically involves dipping the metal in molten zinc or zinc-based coating.

While dangerous if consumed in large quantities, zinc is a micronutrient that plants and humans actually need in small quantities. If too much zinc were leached into the soil, it would probably reflect in dying plants, before it would ever pose a health risk.

Also, galvanized metal has been used to hold or transport water for humans and livestock for many years. All that to say: I can't guarantee there's not a negative health impact, but the risk is certainly low.

A galvanized tub raised bed garden provides a home for herbs and vegetables. (photo: Dennis Huckabay)

One thing you should bear in mind, however, is heat and drainage. Livestock troughs are a popular option, but it's critical to provide lots of drainage holes in the bottom of the trough. That moisture will need a place to escape, so you don't inadvertently drown your plant roots.

Whether you use metal sheeting or a trough, that metal will absorb and reflect heat from the sun – more than other materials. As a result, your soil will tend to dry out more quickly, and foliage in the line of that reflective power might suffer. The soil nearest to the sun-facing metal will also warm up more than the rest of the bed.

It might be wise to plant those tender vegetables – like lettuce – toward the center of the bed where soil temperature will remain most constant.

Tires:

Just don't. Don't do it. If you must do it, do it only for a season or two at most. Tires are a petroleum-based product. Their rubber degrades in the heat and moisture, and the chemicals incorporate into your soil. They may be convenient or look kitschy and fun. It may keep a tire out of the landfill, sure. But there are more drawbacks to using tires than there are benefits.

There's a reason that most landfills prohibit tires. If garbage shouldn't be subjected to decomposing tire rubber, neither should your family's food.

Most landfills prohibit tires. If garbage shouldn't be subjected to decomposing tire rubber, neither should your family's food.

Pre-Made Kits:

It doesn't get much easier than one of the many raised bed kits available for purchase today. These can be used with composite wood and can be cut to varying lengths. Some can be expensive, and the material with which they are made can vary widely. I recently built raised beds on an episode of Growing a Greener World, so check that out.

Liners:

If you use any of the above materials with the potential of leaching, you might be inclined to line the bed with plastic. Yes, this will provide a barrier between the bed material and your soil. But don't lose sight of the plastic material itself.

There are so many plastics out there, and they are of widely-diverse safety grades. If you use plastic, look for food-grade polyethylene. This is considered one of the most food-safe plastics. Line only the outer perimeter of the bed – not the bottom surface. Don't block drainage with plastic.

With all of these products, I recommend you do your own research to feel comfortable in your choice. There are many reputable and not-so-reputable resources out there, so always be mindful of your information resource.

Do the Benefits of Raised Beds Outweigh the Costs?

There are lots of variables to determine if raised beds are your best garden option. Some great gardeners prefer in-ground gardening. A frequent guest of these podcasts gardens in-ground with mounded beds, and he wouldn't have it any other way.

Potential Downsides To Raised Beds:

Their permanence. For most, this is a benefit, but if there's a possibility you will need to relocate your garden in coming years, a permanent raised bed structure will need to be deconstructed.

The raised soil is more exposed to heat and cold than surface soil. If the sidewalls of your bed aren't very thick, the bordering soil and plants could be impacted by extreme conditions.

Raised soil can dry out more quickly than surface soil. During this series, I'll cover some ways to significantly reduce this downside, but the fact remains.

Raised beds require space between the beds for movement, pathways through the garden. If you have a very limited real estate, losing some of it to walking space might be a dealbreaker for you.

Conclusion

Raised garden beds are perfect for novice gardeners and experts alike. They make a garden seem more organized, so there's the visual benefit to keep in mind.But, aside from that, they give more control over soil factors, such as temperature or drainage.